Last Tomato

Jane Ledwell

The Acorn Press
Charlottetown
2005

Last Tomato
ISBN 1-894838-16-5

Editing: John MacKenzie
Author Photo: John Sylvester
Design: Matthew MacKay
Printing: Hignell Printing

The Acorn Press gratefully acknowledges the support of the Prince Edward Island Council of the Arts.

Credits: "Why I Stay" is in *Landmarks: An Anthology of New Atlantic Canadian Poetry of the Land,* Acorn Press, 2001
Earlier versions of "Antipodes" and "Horizon Song" are in *blueSHIFT,* vol.1, issue 1 (1998)
"States of Water" is in the art book (special edition) *Five Poets,* Hazeltree Press and Paper, 2003
"Illuminations" made up part of an installation at the Lunenburg Gallery, NS, 2001

Library and Archives Canada Cataloguing in Publication

Ledwell, Jane, 1972-
Last tomato / Jane Ledwell.

Poems.
ISBN 1-894838-16-5

I. Title.

PS8623.E42L38 2005 C811'.6 C2005-904699-6

ACORNPRESS

The Acorn Press
P.O. Box 22024
Charlottetown, Prince Edward Island
Canada C1A 9J2

www.acornpresscanada.com

For my father,
Frank Ledwell:
teacher, mentor, friend.

Contents

Last Tomato

Overnight, the frost has undone
summer's willful tangle,
leaving tomato plants darkened
to the colour of stopped blood.

My windowsill holds
summer's last tomato.
I'm sorry that at breakfast
mouthful by mouthful
a season's slow burst
will disappear.

Two hundred foreshortened days leave
two hundred dark-lengthened nights to pale
hothouse imitations that might, by the end,
begin to convince us:

because snow comes to mask
the stripped mountain ash
and its last clench of berries,
and some days contain nothing
that is red by its own nature.

Let my tongue speak
the final bloom of memory
so this last bite does not break
faith with time, so its vegetable
sweetness remains
believable, in the moments
you taste my mouth

and let my kiss
flush your cheeks
before the frostburnt wind
can touch you, too.

Berry Season

I.

The first cold morning of August already.
I hang sheets on the line and wonder how long
before cotton gives way to flannel and wool
and dew paints itself to frost against the grass.

Just as I am thinking the choke cherries are ripe,
the grey sky breaks into birds that shake the breeze:
black wave after wave, the sky mirroring the sea, finally.

The birds don't crack their beaks to sing;
they pass with the sound I imagine your skin
would make beneath my fingers: so many birds so
quiet, all that stops day's stillness is this noticing.

When the sky drains, no more birds seem possible,
but more cherry-drunk wings beat the air
and settle in the trees until the woods are rustling
thick and imperceptibly black with birds.

All this, and so soon
after meeting you,
whom I would love.
I would have whispered
into your ear:
to tell you
the whole time
the long grass
was whirring
with crickets.

II.

In the morning.
I wake early, wanting
to ring the brightest chords from your throat.
I hear nothing but the call of crows.

Across your chest, the shadows of a hundred
dark wings, as blackberry-rich as bruises.

Illuminations

Narthex

half a day away
from holding you: only
the black birds know so
far; water pools beneath
where they gather:
predicts weather, skies

Nave

you move
too
thinly
through cor-
ridors
of air

time cools
the sur-
face of
your skin
before
passing

Transept I

you wear a skin like
the walls of an abandoned
building, function seen
through

where love has made you
solid; where collapsed

Choir

a book open
to a page of song

you pry at
closed beaks
for the voices
of birds

Transept II

memory leaves
your farthest parts
hanging fire

smoke lingers
at your nostrils
until you take it
in

Apse

every day
miracles render
what we've never
known or seen

trees point where the wind was going,
morning plumes cold vapour from the river

love blooms from outstretched fingers,
a fragrance that catches
the back of your throat

Singing Instead of Drowning

I. *You Singing*

To sing is to take in enough ocean that you begin to drown;
you invite the sea, only to press it back from your mouth in quick
waves. The thrum of song floats in salt: crests, dips to rake fronds.

The sound washes in, wets the bottoms of shore-borne feet
and strands what it has pried loose from holdfasts
— mermaid hair that tangles ankles in dark, pliable knots.

II. *Fish listening*

Water moves across lateral lines, its touch a fish's listening.
Your swimming, music to the fish's ears.
She, who might be tempted by the fluttering
noise of feathers wrapped around a hooked curve,
a dangerous grace note dangled from the staff of the sky,
will not remember your breath as song, only your
kick and your strange, slow pull towards the air,
towards the silent sun, the gasp of the dry wind.

Why I Stay

because dunes move in stubborn rusting away from rock,
their isthmus kiss closing the mouth of a brackish bay

because at the island's slender throat, strait and gulf can almost
see each other, and desire will someday disintegrate to touch

because the pond's shadow darners weave evening out of trees
and mend the dark path to where northern lights burn rare and possible

because the herons build the marsh from twigs and brine
and sandpipers all together fear the sea's slenderest footfall

because my lungs are calloused with the work of this air,
my hands bruised with the work of this water

because I have already crushed too much stone to red dust
under my feet and I wear all this sand on my tongue

Horizon Song

I have loved you as sure
as mill roads lead to valleys:
so slowly that the mill
might have disappeared
just as you took that last turn
before the bridge.

At the edge of the Island,
ahead is all horizon. Inland,
it is easy to imagine geography
as the only space between us,

but love is known to leave
any landscape, under the arch
of any day-born sky.

For you, I would write
the Prairies I have never seen,
all barley and gold

and grace,
the distant curving of the earth.

Drop to Water

Once I lived on an island so far from other landfall
birds turned flightless in face of the ocean.

I pressed between the wind and moon —
back to the wind, face to the moon — wondering
if the wind that pushed and the moon that pulled
both knew the dark drop to water ahead.

The blind wind throws birds ahead of it,
flings winged diviners from point to point,
flight finally lodging in their instincts,
a migration past vision, fear, darkness.

Here I press between the wind and moon again,
back to the wind, face to the moon, feet wet
on a cold collapse of sand. Have I flown?
Did I fall? Will I turn to land again?

Antipodes

It takes an Australasian a long time to see colour in the Canadian landscape. We're used to a more lurid palette.
— M. H., New Zealand

I think of my ancestors' long learning, the generations
before Thomson saw the crimson grasp of jackpines,
Carr cracked the beating human heart of the woods.

You and I walk against a slow-moving sky,
its clouds furrowed down long ploughed rows.
This October is summer that has forgotten spring,
a winter stripped of its white.
Wind shapes sand into new hills overnight;
tilled soil turns up potatoes.

At the shore, you think sandpipers are the smallest birds
you have ever seen, so I tell you a hummingbird,
a green thumb suspended.
But it is past migration. There is no green to measure against.

I think of you conjuring a hummingbird's invisible wing.

And I remember your country as if I had seen it in slides,
as light through the selected stills.
Driving north to summer was all green: growth
lush with the remembered fire
of volcanoes. Green water. Green lawns.

Beside the motorway, the sheep-mowed hills
looked lonely for the bush.
But I learned such relief in dull orange soil
spilling from their gashed slopes,
I would have cut them with my own knife.

Oamaru, New Zealand: 45°S

In memory of Janet Frame, 1924–2004

This isn't how it happened, but it's true:
You left the country for home, so I left town —
went where I thought I was going anyway,
to Oamaru. It could have struck
at any moment, and, finally, it did.
The light failed in two seasons at once.

Facing north and west, I took a picture of home,
invisible across an ocean forever only
as pacific as the next storm. I wanted to show
you a faint prism arced at the horizon, but it
didn't photograph. I knew I'd have to
remember it all the way back to town.

First, I found the cliffs where dusk-waddling
penguins came ashore in twos. I watched from a shelter
that gave no shelter, where binoculars rimmed my
eyes with cold. Wet lenses blurred the far
view down; water bent the scene into wavering
circlets, stretching the edge of sand, blurring rock.

Sparse yellow-eyed penguins were moving
white bellies and yellow eyes rising so quickly
up sheer cliff paths they might forget flightlessness.
Farther down coast, fairy penguins landed
in a grey huddled herd. Tourists watched from bleachers.
Locals cursed the wasted fish smell.

I thought I was looking for someplace I had
read in books, for an author who had suffered
to the edge of the world, for her demolished house
regrown into cabbage trees, a grassy mound
where a hollow once formed a foundation: distant from
the town, where limestone buildings glared old ostentations.

The sun sank across empty years and unpeopled streets.
and all the insides lit with artificial fire that burns down
carbons to the weight of foregone expectation.
In Oamaru, I was for one night again where I had already
been (on the far side of the world): it could have been halfway
from somewhere imagined or halfway from somewhere cold.

Moving West

It took four years to get to Sudbury's stripped, ugly land.

No wonder we're too tired to try for Thunder Bay.

You're moving west (a shifting point),
and though I am moving you,
your vehicle is unphrased desire,
the curve of his lashes under breath from your mouth,
the dream of you curled into the ideal, for once.

You and I, we give men years to come around to loving us.

You always said he'd never leave her,
and on the road you know he never will,
and in the bright and sudden loss of him,
you think of settling somewhere off the highway,
near Elliot Lake — perhaps the Boychuk Road.

But the Canadian Shield holds on to history,
so we drive from the Chippewa down to find remnants,
proofs in pictographs on sheer faces,
hard-fought old visions we reach for, feet bare,
hips girded to rock that mocks our short skirts.

Superior, looking up, pretends it wouldn't swallow our
presumptions whole.

Ontario ends hours after the novelty of muskeg wears out,
and we know again it was the word we had wanted,
the word from the story of steam-driven engines,
stopped dead where tracks lapsed into geological time.

In Manitoba, who knew there would be beach to sleep on,
a lake that could have been an ocean (you could see that far),
and over the land-locked lake, the moon risen higher

and broader than we'd ever seen,
looking harder for tidal water.

We wake to find yellow-headed blackbirds are after all just that,
painting their names across marshlands
in a horizontal bulrush waltz,
recalling flashing epaulettes of red-winged blackbirds
we know from our own ocean.

Near Portage la Prairie with the whole plain ahead, east is over our shoulder.

Saskatchewan, and the car begins to smell
of memory and other dead things,
so we burn the roses from the lover you left,
mingle dry thorns and wild roses,
light petals with sagebrush from the continent's plateau
beside blinding canola.

We drive easily off the map, drawn by a mountain of potash we can't say how to use.

In Alberta, you think you should have known
by the badlands that the floor can cave right out,
that extinction happens when bones least expect it,
and you never know where they will show
up from under the earth.

You know only love could have crushed the continent this slowly into mountains.

You know because you have never seen them before.

British Columbia is all downhill in third gear
with a foot near the brake for ten hours;
we have no idea how far up we are.

Though we're not high enough
that it should be snowing now
snow spins the trees around us,
flakes so big they could be blossoms,
the sky so grey they could be soot.

We pray not to die where the country is rushing to its endings.

We arrive in a city you've never seen
where you will now live,
and you know pacific weather
will make every pathetic fallacy true,
since it will rain every day you are with him
and every day that you are not.

It will take moons on the far side
of the pointed mountains to realize
love triangles are about the angles,
not the lines of force that bind the points.

You've driven as straight a line as the country allows.

You will still face east where your body tells you an ocean,
and when you turn your back to the cold,
you will only have America.

The moon will birth waves onto a shore that's never been smitten
with water.

The unwashed sand will surprise at the chill.

The ocean will tell you that coasts are not endings.

Intertidal

Blue shells and remnants
in June pockets, held against the grey
to see me through the year.
Set in windowsills,
shells filled with pebbles.
Patient. (You filled my waiting.)

I thought islands had edges,
until I saw an ocean through its seasons.

Fall winds unearth bone and shell,
press sand into inlets, pull spruce to precipice
where the land's last thrust buttressed itself with trees.

Winter brings back peninsulas: snows that knew
an ice age return to extend the land past sight,
to make maquettes of earth's cooling crust, plates crushing
each other, a hastening geologic grind.

I saw spring remake the present, restore water's vastness into
a puzzle more and more unsolvable under the sun.

Walked the intertidal sand in summer;
you thought it ended there.

States of Water

But to imagine an individual soul for each and any starlet of snow is utterly absurd, and therefore the shapes of snowflakes are by no means to be deduced from the operation of soul in the same way as with plants.

—Johannes Kepler, 1611

I. *The Morphology of the Invisible*

If you can see it, it is not steam;
it is mist, already falling.
Though you sense its density,
Steam is the prickle, not the sweat.

It takes energy to disappear.

Clouds collect the day's evanescence, return it to earth.
Do souls gathered into the sky eventually descend?
After the phase changes of the body,
what phase changes the soul?

II. *The Crystallography of Ice*

This is the structure of grief:
the crystalline form of water.

Transfixed in the inevitable bonds of design,
the hexagonal prisms of creed,
hollow in the interstices.

Emptiness brings such lightness:
cod driven into waters too cold float to the surface,
their gills spread like hands reaching for comfort.
Dendrites drill, explode the soft cell.
This is the ordinary order of nature.

This ice, this grief: like a soul in its singularity,
it invades the architecture of the body.
The chest filled with air: the gasp taken in, not released;
The final heave of the frozen earth before sublimation.

III. *Melting point, freezing point*

Zero, exactly, is the point
ice and water coexist;
not freezing, not melting,
fixed in being unbecoming.

Less than zero, and freeze spreads.
Slow — molecule by molecule —
watch it, through its own latticework,
assemble itself: lace winding from
the bobbins of temperature and pressure.

More than zero, an nth of degree,
and ice slips its structure and vanishes
into water; the warmth a sudden catastrophe.

That a moment of zero and a moment of flood
exist in the same minute, the same day
explains the murmur of the south wind,
its whispers barely discerned
after the north wind's soapbox shout.

Listen to the coaxing spin in the southern gust
and hear the soaking rhetoric of homogeneity.

IV. *The symmetry of liquid water*

Does water retain its symmetry in translation,
or like language, is it broken when fixed
and refixed against the platen glass of syntax?

When we carry ice as a lightness, water as a weight.
Who can tell us what is given, what taken?
Water is its own wholeness: however much there is,
that is its total — half empty, half full.
Half visible, half disappeared.

The symmetry of liquid water is
the same disorder from any angle.

Earth

After the Columbia *disaster, February 2002*

We sit erect in wooden pews at the funeral,
our spines straight as steeples, as ringed
by time as the trees that grew the wood.

The church, in cross-section, is
a rocket poised for lift-off;
our braced bodies anticipate g-forces.

Oh, the rush of leaving earth.

This June funeral is years too early.
I am ashamed at tears I have not earned,
for a cousin only known and loved by blood.

And little one, I tried to tell you
(in my belly, small and whole as a world,
feeling my every breath contract into a sob):
there is more on earth than crying,
there is more on earth than death.

As the priest cast a handful of clay across the casket
I tried to tell you its redness under sunshine,
the ruddy cast the dust left on his living hand.

I could not convince you,
and you passed from me too soon,
pulled by gravity, but never touching earth.

You would have been born the February
that began with unplanned fireworks,
astronauts exploding on attempted reentry.
They blazed and were scattered
across a country preparing rockets for war.

Little one, you knew to be afraid.
There is no good time to come to earth.

Covenant

In the stubble field a ladder grows.
I climb until hung between earth and sky.

The ladder continues.

The earth turns to water, and I climb higher, see farther
to my parents' barn, down the slope to the brook,
across the valley's deepest fissure, where a swath
of trees has been mown and replanted in pressure-
treated telephone poles, power lines.

I look down into the nests of birds, but as I lean
into them, the ladder leans, too, and I see
it is not built of wood, but of tied silk scarves. It slumps
towards the water. I reach up, it is raining.

Water rushes up and down,
the firmament broken, the covenant undone.

Things Apart

My father knows the cut of wildflowers,
the dandelion secret: roots of wine and coffee.
He calls the black-eyed susans to box the wind, fight upright.

> (And mayflowers hold the ground —
> breathe earth, perfume.)

My mother knows the feel of bread, grain flour:
the knead that opens white welcome spaces.
She builds around absences, oven-warm, yeasty.

> (These sing hollow beneath the crust —
> invite a touch, a tap.)

They know things apart; they know things into pieces.

They take the measure of summer, permeable days,
short nights when light draws back its skin at dusk.
Their doors open into enclosures of woods, of words.

> (They say: carry this hammer,
> know the heaviness of promises.)

In This Climate

When we were born
into the fierce climate of love,
we did not choose our names
but borrowed them from earth
frozen around the bones of our mothers'
dreamed-of children,
our fathers' never-born lovers.

In this climate, leaves are gone
longer than we know them;
trees stay alive from their roots.
What they lose (moisture, verdure) is from the surface.
They do not say what they guard when they give up
their last colour in the struggle against frost.

I love trees more for knowing their branches.
No wonder I cannot leave winter for long.

So much of what I hold for you is under
the cold casuistry of words,
in the autonomic emptying
chambers of heart and lungs.

What's insulated we call temperate.
No surprise we desire to rename constellations
for things more fixed and stable than gods:
love, jealousy, rage, history.

Dogs know you leave your scent in snow;
it blooms to leaves, grass,
your grandmothers' lost breath.

March Storm

Have you, too, slept burrowed in snow?
Wakened with breath the colour and texture of sky?

Messenger, ice has stolen the heat from your wingtips
so you can't caution others that wind in snow-clogged eavestroughs
sings a false course home, that a spring-loaded storm casts cold
across hollows, drifts collapse the colour of dusk,
fill the graves of November's lost sparrows.

March, awkward first robin, never flew.
No, for months she nested under snow, underground,
burnishing her breast and heart to rust and flame
until thaw released this early shudder of her wings,
a slow rising of earth's deep warmth, a warning.

Harrow

under the brows of black-eyed men,
memory ringed with years nothing grew

the red land weeps its own rusting;
it does not promise kindness

weather draws iron from under red lacquer
to rejoin the soil, layers sorrow on loss

this land harbours too much,
grasps at passing breezes

what a combine spins to gold gets harrowed
back to rust until it claims the harrower

soil carried on the backs of foxes
past the snow-lined gutter of the woods

dust on the cheeks of squirrels
in the nested hearts of trees

For Emily

When she was young, she thought
tears would stain her face forever,
leaving thick, white streaks like scars.
Her swollen lids held sadness in.
The crumbling damp behind her eyes
left her vulnerable to cold.

One night she froze and woke up broken.
When she found her lips and teeth, she said
she had wandered all night where the cold was,
north and threatening, and everything turned
brittle: the pond, rushes, ice-trapped limbs.

In a thaw, her eyes might spring
for the frogs that break their throats
where she once ate raisins as
we picnicked in the snow,
before the brimming night swallowed.

Berry Picking

Hills spread to level heights,
roll from haze to valley.
Her brow rises to gray wisps;
half-blind, hip-deep in a brambled ditch
she is picking blueberries,
round and ripe and full

White berry:
too soon picked stays
shut tight and strong
as her big-boned house that opened
with smells of near-done sausages
and liver left over and over

Green berry:
her kitchen linoleum was a universe,
white with green constellations, the centre
a giant star of square green tiles
where children orbited — so many satellites

Half ripe:
they overran her yard on two wheels
each gathering bruises, aching
to dark purple-seamed red:
glistened round and sore
under the dew-glaze of water

Blue berry:
rolls down to the hollows from the mound
she builds in her bowl, clings to leaves
like dirt to knees low to the ground

She:
covered in blue powder,
round and ripe and full:
hip-deep, near deaf to so much
laughter, children spilling
blueberries from half-filled cups
as they spin and whirl
through the morning-green world,
and brambles

Grandmother

On the couch, her children's children pile
snowdrift high into each others' laps,
they are so plenty, and their legs tangle
halfway across the room with all their growing.
She taught them to rely on cousins.

If you don't have family to fall back on,
nobody'll have you.

She's visiting today from the nursing home,
where her grown children sit in daily shifts to guard her
against losing the name that's taped to her door
and sewn to her underwear.

She worries her hem and says, "All these bodies,
and none of them my own."
She dreams a path aloud to Maple Plains,
and it's God knows when again.

The cousins watch old photographs for change.
Memory chases them across the pages.
They look for themselves, mostly —
here straightened and combed into scowls,
there wild-tongued laughing into tickles —
and they touch their faces to check
for blemishes long-since vanished.

Grandmother disappears again into marriage
and labours that repeat longer than memory.
The tall-shouldered boys with their lank, shifting limbs
make her hands twitch for loaves of bread to knead,
make her knees bend under the weight of a cast-iron
kettle that cannot be full enough for all of them.

She calls her daughters by their wrong names,
and when they don't hear, she worries in their direction
and hopes the boys will go back to work
in the fields when they are taken care of.

To settle her, the cousins share papered memories.
She nods and nods at all the gloss.
The two-dimensioned pictures miss
the last dimension of her time-slipped mind.

Living uses the length and breadth of her days,
leaving only depth to memory,
depth missing in the flat-pressed collections
of arms and heads and feet she sees
as clouded arrangements of colour, stranger to her
than the cousins who move noisy around her chair
through ageless space, unclaimed.
Unclaimed.

Cemetery, St. Peter's Bay

I.

How do we grieve an expected death,
its heartbeats heard, heard, heard, unheard?

Except moment by moment,
as grass inclines under the drop of water
or sighs beneath the restless silence of the gust;
except by giving way to mercy as the sky gives way to blue.

Each moment clings, a burr on my perception, its hooks
grown because it gave up on wind when wind was gone.

II.

Our families waited one by one for a break
and marked it in the earth with their shovels
and at their heads with their stones
(for some, the only earth they'd ever own:
the infants, the girls, poor queer cousin Alec).

Our dead lie together on the side of a hill on the edge of a bay,
their names rotting side by side since before our conception;
they grow, a field of granite mushrooms that love
the shore and the earth's putrefaction.

The bay fills with the run-off of the dead.
My father remembers how they choked off his childhood
with eelgrass that binds swimmers' feet.

Mussel barges ferry food from this world,
feed the dead to the living.

III.

The dead are not gone: they push
absence into protuberance,
every hill a midden,
deaths stacked like cordwood
against every house,
heaped like sand under the
daggers of grass rising
from gnarled digits that
clutch into the earth,
kneading the dead.

IV.

Fall, in desperation, confesses everything:
          the blood of leaves
          the pallid, crooked bones of trees
          the land gashed by summer

All of it asks absolution.

Light beads out sorrowful mysteries,
hard grey berries that clump to bay bushes.

But the old scourge of weather,
the thin growl of the cruelest bird,
grackles inchoate sounds,
reciting the sins of the unforgiven.

V.

My love, our deaths will be separate.
Death pulls things from us in pieces.

> (I have felt this.
> Deaths can pass
> through a woman's body
> leaving her thin, alone.
> Ask her where her children are.
> She will say they float.)

Pull back the sand, and in the shallow
impression your body has made
tears brim from the earth.
Other wells are too deep
for the consolation of water.

Where are our dead who are not drowned?
Where are our dead who are not scattered?
Where are our dead who are not in the ground?
Where but here?

Odd Petals

Come mid-summer, we hold all flowers as our own.

Goldenrod knows all that glitters is hammered thin by August.
Alchemical summer gathers gold into the day's eye
and radiates odd petals we use to decipher love.

Fireweed flares where fire has never passed, fooled again
by the susans' scorched eyes, the flame-fringed paintbrushes,
the overheated drip of butter and eggs.

Thistles burr; dandelions burst mouthfuls of feathers.
Clover funnels nectar from the wind, leaving salt in the spray
for wild roses that gape and loll their tongues where even
wind can bruise them, let alone the cut and thrust
nightshade that ripens to poison.

Spotted touch-me-nots lick at the rain, lap at the dew,
and hang loose-lipped, watching water facet itself to jewels.
Tangles of purple vetch clutch handful after handful
of the ditch's wet rolling hip.

If our blooming's too late, love, consider seconds pass
fraction by fraction slower than our hearts beat.

A Temporary Kiss

I. *A Compliment (The Art of the Possible)*

If any praise is worth meeting with praise
(halfway, where tongues entangle)
then your mouth has set a trap for my breath.

I would take you as a lover, if I could unleash my love
in sound across space to where you trill melodies
my heart remembers from prayers.

If there were anything I could offer that you could accept,
it would crack open the generosity of the universe
where it first slit into stars.

We would know
        the blank miracle of hands,
        the branded love of moths.

II. *St. Agnes's Eve*

On St. Agnes's Eve, when a maiden waits for signs, I get
  a full moon
   a lunar eclipse
    a blizzard
     a flood tide

In the storm is desire already past remembering
        when the land is buried in a smooth white line
        that burns bare-fingered touch?

Why now do I lose the knack for divination
        when the sea presses its teeth to the mouth of the harbour
        and floods all the basements of the world?

III. *Morning*

You wake with a blade to the throat of the day,
afflicted by a persistence of love,
homeless with the thought of every
thing you could never want
enough.

I want to kiss you exactly
where your coiled wire mind meets the friction of skin,
where scars mark you as your own,
I want your orphaned soul, your widowed body,
all the small ardours of your mouth.

In half-light, shape my lips to the question
that has been forming,
a beginning that gathers
all your endings
into this one.

Apologia

I.

We call each other
my darling, my dear.

Such is the intimacy of names
that to speak the syllables
conferred by water, confirmed by habit
brings us too close
within the confines of our every day.

We do not know what our names might call down from our natures.

Such is your heaviness on my tongue:
you will be a name left burned into rock.

II.

We walk slowly on sand
as if to name every grain we can see.
But fire could make of the grains one pane:
a cataract.

III.

You shudder at the sudden blindness of the end,
I, the vision of an end beginning.

You fear the fall of fire because you are afraid to die.
I, afraid to live
without.

I speak of the past because it is done with.
You are silent for the same reason.
We are both sorry.

Detail

I.

you speak
a tongue that ripples
intelligible through
my muscles:
sound
waves
striking
a drum

II.

memory absorbs
the shock of lips:
bruises surface
from another life

III.

any kiss
would break
through me
crest and roll
with a pull-
back under-
tow,
shores
collapsing
as if sand
never held

Geologic

We've called it clay too long,
this earth we're formed of,
shaped to its definition.

But this red earth is not clay
to be turned on the wheel,
to be cupped in potters' hands,
to carry to our mouths dregs of boiled tea.

Not elastic when moist, not solid when fired:
its sandy crumble is touch's truer science,
though not sand enough to burn to glass,
to seek another form that holds.

Summer speaks the febrile
delirium of naming.

We have spoken long enough of origins with this accent
that describes language moving through
the earth where we were born.

North Shore

The black bird hooks his beak out of the cliff face,
wings clipped into stone.
Witness every night to what he already knows.

Midnight falls over the tide,
water swells minutely.

A lap at the shore, but ocean holds
its tension in the far arc of a meniscus,
draws away from its edges, plumps its core.

The waves reflect the moon's intent,
one line of light aligned, sublime, with every eye.

A waver.

You, too, stood on the north shore, with bareknuckled trees
fighting god. Did you know?
Over the ocean, all along, the moon wanted salt, not water.

Of Fishers, of Men

A walk on the water a wet distance from home,
    born to a fisher where the day breaks.

A window on woe in a boatless season,
    born to the shore where the water breaks.

An easement afloat with a ballast of stone,
    born to the man where the voice breaks.

A breakwater pulse, reckoning with order, a collision with sea,
    born to the heart where land breaks.

Miracle days. Loaves alone. The end of a closed house;
    the crest of a breaking wave.

Mind of Winter

I.

creation's unfinished and god is still resting;
blackbirds gossip all day of what's left to be done

II.

spruces draw us in, their charcoal hearts visible:
trees embraced by white birds, their wings the shape of snow

III.

plowed fields release colour to show birds the wind:
how its blades hedgerow paths for the flight of snow

IV.

that fluid edge of distance may just be water:
and in winter, it is — leaving us to dig bridges

V.

black branches hold the night all day against the sun;
dusk falls: the slowest passion of the horizon

Three Rural Routes

I. *Pentecost: Valley Road*

You drive us down a lane
hidden by its closeness to the road,
to a valley rippling with noise,
water running down its own making.

Below terraced clouds, the sky blurs with heat.
Raptors rise, potent with fire: then
turn down, release a rush of upward air
A kingfisher cuts straight, truer
than water, across the hawks' circling gaze.

Again, you've taken me somewhere unexpected.
Tonight, when the sky closes and the land cools,
you will search for paths you still don't know,
as though you've lived here all your life.

II. *Lent: Shore Road*

Salt water still clenched in ivory, silent,
teeth of ice, broken at the harbour.
Whether by nature or by force, we can't tell.

The beach is gone and all its sand drowned —
though the sea will reject it, with all the dead.
Sand will insinuate any old place.

I want to ask the fox (pregnant, wary):
Where will sea and wind allow us
to take our ease, when ice recedes?

When I wake one day to find your red pelt
paled to the grey-gold of winter grass,
freckled skin diminished in the sun.

Oh, the bowl of your sternum, the lift of your cheek,
the knotweed cord of your tendons,
to wash finally ashore where bones bleach.

Spring begins here, beneath the bridge,
at the mouth of the path where the harbour opens.
We don't know how it will end.

III. *Easter: Village Road*

The churches have all let out.

Where we drive I see only the dead —
their houses limn the highway.

Parents lost a province away while children slept safe.
Lovers crashed into a dark curve.
A strong-armed boy drawn by a midnight current.
A man with a ladder he would not climb.
A woman, tired from the work of sons, sleeping deep
    into a prayer for peace.

Strange, the frames and wooden skins
of lives stand unmarked by grief.

I don't know why I see them.
They are not my dead,
and this is not country you know.

You are noticing the shapes
snow drifts, the bird that lights
on shadow and leaves
no shadow itself. You think,
"It is the living that rise."

The road we drive is short.

But the people from here would know
what I am remembering,
would say they know
just where we drove,
where we turned
to come back.

Bedsheet

On the line
the sheet holds the curve
of your back
out of habit (it has held you
all winter)
until a breeze snaps it flat.

It stretches back, restless,
slouched and then supine,
bracing warp against weft,
remembering in its cells
the twist of its growing
as it arches towards the sun
that twined its fibres.

Muscle and sinew
crack with exertion.

So we all aspire to our own shapes,
the shapes that we wake into —

though the curl that held me inside
my mother may be the same shape
I cling around your tight heart.

Acknowledgments

This book would not be possible without my incredible family of creative and challenging people: my mother Carolyn, my father Frank, my siblings Emily, Patrick, Thomas, Daniel, and Christian, and their partners Tara and Isabelle.

I am grateful to the Prince Edward Island Council of the Arts for support during the creation of this manuscript. I thank my editor, John MacKenzie, for pressing for so long for these poems to become a manuscript and then working with me to shape them into a book. I thank my publisher, Laurie Brinklow, for her courage and commitment in publishing local books.

Many of these poems have been read and critiqued by family, friends, and peers in writing groups, workshops, and more casual settings. I thank all of the people who have come in contact with them and shared their insights. I also thank those who have shared their lives with me with such generosity.

And I thank Stephen, who is better than anything I ever asked for or expected.